Positive Next Steps

Thought Provoking Messages to Move in a New Direction

Gina M. D'Amore-Nisco
LSC, CSMC, CCWC, IEC

DEDICATION

This book is dedicated to my children, Brittany, Robert, and Thomas, since I have dedicated my life to them, and I hope they will always know, without question, that they are loved.

ACKNOWLEDGMENTS

I publicly want to thank my parents for bringing me into this world and teaching me morals, values, and ethics, before anyone else did. They were the first people to show me what love is, and that with perseverance; I can shape my future to be a positive journey. I continue living that way daily. Although miles separate us, my love for you both only grows stronger, and I am grateful for you.

Thank you to my grandparents for the wisdom that only they could provide. I learned many things from their journey especially from the "Grain." She still continues at 95 years young, to amaze me with her cooking skills and her strength, (don't believe me, place her in front of a slot machine and watch out), but most of all her love. You always will be a part of my heart.

Thanks to my sister Denise and my brothers Carmine and Vincent. We were like most siblings and had our share of arguments and nonsense but also fun times. I must say that I love each of you for who you are and for the great memories that we share. In addition, to Joanne and Lisa, my sister-in-laws, for the love you show to my brothers and our family.

Thank you to Frank, my husband of twenty-one years, who was there for me and with me through many great times but also some tragedies. I will always have love and respect for you and will always be thankful for the three greatest gifts we gave each other, Brittany, Robert, and Thomas.

Brittany - you will always be my dancing princess and any opportunity that I am able to watch you is always a highlight for me. You are energetic, smart, talented, and my beautiful daughter. I wish nothing but continued success for you.

Robert - you have always been intelligent, handsome, and thoughtful. The world is your oasis on many levels, so continue to never let opportunities pass you by. Keep those visions burning bright, and never lose your great laugh.

Thomas - you have excelled at ice hockey that it still amazes me to watch you at your games. You are a handsome, young man with a kind soul. Always stay positive, and never stop learning. Follow your dreams and stay compassionate.

Alexandria – you have the potential to do great things, so find that deep within you, and follow through. Stay focused on raising your son Noah whom we all love very much. Teach him to have a zest for life and learning.

Thank you to Leo who was there for me when it was time to begin again and is there with me as I continue to move forward. We share a love and passion for life that has enabled both of us to turn our lives around.

Daniel – you have made great strides in your life. Your sense of curiosity defines you at times so keep that passion in a positive light. Stay focused and treasure the bond we have.

Thomas – you have a sense of humor and quick wit that is very refreshing. I hope you never harden your heart.

Joseph - you have the courage and ability to meet your goals. Achieve greatness without excuses.

Moreover, to my extended family and friends, I love each one of you and will continue to cherish any time I have to spend with you!

PREFACE

I am very humbled to all that have directly and indirectly influenced me. This book is a compilation of statements and messages that I have given to my clients throughout the last decade. I have been told that it was my words that changed their lives. Therefore, I have put together some of my most thought provoking messages with a desire that you, too, will make a Positive Next Step.

I hope that as you read the following pages, you will be able not only to live more positively but also to love more positively. This is and always will be my goal.

Change is a constant in everyone's life, but most of us never know how to move passed simple complaints. These complaints about how one feels, or about repeating the same old behaviors, continue to produce unhappy, yet familiar results. Clinging on to self-pity is always counterproductive. Therefore, adopt a willingness to change, and have the courage to do so.

Recognize that there are not *quick fixes* to figure out what is next, but that you, and only you, have the ability to make the changes desired to meet your goals. Become goal oriented, and build confidence in yourself so that you can come up with the solutions that fit your life.

~ Be responsible for what happens to you ~

Nothing in this world is ever impossible. We choose to accept either that we are not good enough or that we cannot do something without ever giving it a chance. We are afraid of change! We allow negativity to keep us from moving on. Impossibility becomes a way to live; however, if you take the time to envision what you want to accomplish, you will surprise yourself with new thoughts of possibility.

What is keeping you from making things happen? Are you really that closed minded to think you are not capable of living out your dreams? Open your mind, and allow your conscious thoughts to see the possibilities that lie ahead of you. You have the knowledge, and the power, to make the impossible possible. It may be hard at first, but, over time and with an attainable attitude, you will achieve this. Take the first two letters off impossible. Now, how do you feel?

~ POSSIBLE ~

Our everyday life is comprised of choices that we make and do not make. We hope that we always make the right decisions. Since we are not perfect, chances are we will have regrets. The problem with that is that regrets can have a very powerful effect on us when we allow them to surface. Our negative experiences tend to stick with us, which can sustain a hold on us that is impossible to escape. We let ourselves become burdened down with the weight of regret, and we live a vicious cycle without realizing that we can let go.

All the divorces I have mediated, through the years, have been full of regrets on both sides. I tell my clients it is now time to make peace with yourself. Allow yourself to learn from your mistakes, but, at the same time, do not continue to carry the burden of the negative thoughts that go along with regrets. This will never be productive to you or those around you. Rather, face the burdens and the emotional baggage, so this inner turmoil will begin to fade away. Let yourself know that it is okay to be imperfect, so you can stop beating yourself up. Allow inner peace to take over.

~ Make peace with your regrets ~

So many of us live in the past never realizing that life is always changing. What we did even a second ago will never be as it was. We run the same scenarios over and over in our minds. We wish we could go back to relive the good times, and erase the bad ones. Time then becomes wasted on the past.

Remember, life is a constant series of changes, and, with growth, we see that life will never be what it was. Embrace this! Instead of fighting for the past, put all that effort into your present day. Learn to focus on your future endeavors, and keep your past as your history.

~ Make every day count ~

We will encounter problems, at different phases, in our lifetime. It is how we choose to handle them that make us grow and enjoy our life. How many times have you heard from family and friends that they live every day in a world of problems? They are forever complaining how their life is so negative, and nothing goes their way. They lose sight that they have the power to make their life more beneficial.

The first step is to turn your problems into solutions. Do not stay in your own world merely existing. Instead, begin to live. Problems should be taken as opportunities to create a better life for you. Wake up each day ready to make positive changes, so you can embrace life and all that it has to offer. There are hidden solutions all around you, but it is up to you to find them and to focus on the positive aspects. The choice is ALWAYS up to you.

~ Make it happen ~

So many people feel they have the right to tell others, continually, what is wrong with them as if it is their job to do so. They carry on and on about what that person should or should not be doing. Being presumptuous makes you arrogant, causes disrespect, and allows you to take authority that you do NOT have!

Be confident without being presumptuous. You have no idea what that person is going through, or what they have been through, so knock it off. It is always better to have a humble heart, great attitude, and kindness for others. That will always go further than presumption ever will!

~ Do not be a know it all ~

We will receive messages from others signaling that we need to make a change. However, we continue as if *we* are not the problem. I hear wives say to their husbands, "You don't talk to me or listen to anything I have to say." I hear husbands exclaim, "She never has time for me," and the list grows. These are warning signs to one another that there is a disconnect in the relationship, and it is time to make a change. Most of us tend to ignore these with a *whatever* attitude, and continue as if they do not exist. Eventually, our life is full of frustration and resentment.

It is time to reverse that way of thinking, and time for YOU to make the change necessary to live a more fulfilled life. Do not wait for others to make a change, since that is holding your life back from being all that it can be. Take your own responsibility towards living a productive and genuine life on a daily basis. Understand that these warning signs exist and are very real.

~ Make these changes now, so your journey will become more complete ~

Having a positive attitude allows you to see the good you have and not focus on what you do not have. Gratitude also follows, since you appreciate your life and not feel miserable thinking you should have more than what you already have. Thanklessness is a cruel cycle considering it can cause undue stress to you. Negative stress, as we all know, is not good for anyone.

The point is, no matter what, having a positive attitude will allow you to live in the present day. This affords you the opportunity not to miss the joys that come into your life. We do not get a second chance to enjoy what each day brings to us.

~ Treasure life and pass it forward ~

I believe that respect is something that needs to be earned. I cannot tell you the number of times, especially when I mediate divorces, this term is thrown around between parties as if demanded. However, in order for you to have someone respect you, you must be willing to respect the other person. We respect others by meeting their needs, voluntarily, as well as considering their feelings. When these considerations are met, you earn the respect of the other person.

Hence, do not demand that others respect you while you continue on a negative path or one of being self-righteous. Rather, validate and empathize with others in a sincere way. See what you can do to teach others that when you give respect, you get respect. Believe in your heart, and in your head, that people have feelings that need to be validated and not turned away. Being different is part of life, and, in spite of everything, everyone has a right to be respected for who they are.

~ **Give respect to get respect** ~

"I cannot do this because it is too hard," "I do not know how to forgive." These are only two very common examples of excuses that people tend to use. Have you ever been in a situation that requires you to go the extra mile, or do something out of your *comfort zone*? When tough times occur, do you handle it with excuses or in a positive manner?

Do not stay on the negative side allowing your thoughts to keep you from moving forward. Excuses are counterproductive! You need to realize that you do have the power to get through rough times. Find something that you can appreciate, and make your mind up to stay decisive. The results are amazing when you make this your mindset. Never give up.

~ This journey is up to you, and, by pressing through, you will achieve greatness without any excuses ~

No one wants to be criticized. When we see or hear that word, it immediately conjures up a negative thought process. Our brains process this negative feedback in a form of resentment and defensiveness.

Since criticism is always a part of our lives, it is important for us to learn to take that negativity and turn it into something positive. Easier said than done at times; however, you can decipher what is being said to you because of your actions and not necessarily you as a person. Look at the actions that are being spoken of, and, if possible, improve them. Do not let it become a personal attack and then attack back at the attacker. Detach yourself emotionally so you do not stoop to that level.

~ **Always be the better person** ~

Too often, people treat others with such indifference as if their life is the only one that is important. A couple at the grocery store spoke to the cashier as if her life was worthless, and she was only there to service their needs. When asked a simple question by the cashier, the woman rudely said, "Oh right, you could not possibly figure that out, since this is all you can do in life and probably never even graduated." As I watched this unfold, ready to interject, the cashier politely replied, "Oh right, you could not possibly figure out that I hold an MBA but chose this line of work after I was laid off from my position as an operations manager. But, I do continue to be a productive member of society!" At that point, the couple did not say another word. In my mind, I knew that they did not learn anything from this, although I held out hope. I was next in line, so I said to the cashier, "I'm sorry that happened, but I loved how you brought it all to life." She questioned why so many people act like that. I explained that those people do not know what compassion is, and they act as if their life is all that matters.

Compassion is very powerful! It teaches you that no matter where you are in life, all of us have a story. By putting up walls, you may miss some great people. Do not just look for those who can give you what you want, rather, be an advocate. Furthermore, look for those that you can help. Reach out to those with a smile, a thank you, a warm hello, but, most importantly, have compassion for others always.

~ Do not be judgmental; try being compassionate ~

Why is it that we feel entitled to our way at times? There will always be individual differences and disagreements in relationships. Why should one person be allowed to think they have the greater authority?

Try making agreements rather than feel entitled. Entitlements are awarded to oneself, whereas agreements are brought about with the consent of all parties involved. This way no one is feeling left out, and the relationship is made of mutual consent.

~ Our wants should not be a right ~

Have you fallen into the trap of self-pity? You allow certain situations to overtake you and begin to give up on future goals. This, eventually, leads you to miss issues pertinent not only to your future but to your life in the present. Consequently, you lose yourself and all that life may present to you.

Therefore, do not define yourself by self-pity. We all go through situations and experiences that make us feel like giving up, at times, as we stay stuck in this spiral state. Giving up will always affect you adversely. Rather than allowing that to happen, control the situation with solutions that make a positive change. Learn to adapt.

~ Take control of your life ~

How often are you playing the *blame game*? "I went to work late again today because my boss hates me." "My teacher is so annoying giving us all this homework, so I am not going to do it." "My wife is always criticizing me, so why bother." Moreover, the list goes on and on. All of these are excuses not to put our best foot forward, and to find fault in others, instead of looking at our own life to see what needs to change. It is always much easier to find a way to blame someone else for our unhappiness and to live in a world that is **all about me**.

It is time to take responsibility, and OWN your life without placing your unhappiness on others. The teacher is not annoying because homework is assigned. You do not want to be bothered with it, so you blame him or her. The boss does not hate you, but, perhaps, is not pleased with your **always-late** appearance, rightfully so. Hence, you continue to blame your laziness and lack of being there on time on the boss. As for relationships, stop looking at the other party as if they are the one who is always wrong or the nagging one. It takes two of you to make a relationship work, and neither person is ever going to be perfect. Realize what it is that you are contributing instead of blaming your partner for your lack luster in life. Recognize what your actions are before playing the *blame game,* and own up to them. Be accountable for your wrongdoings. In doing so, it leads to open and honest communication without a false sense of self.

~ Stop the excuses ~

From the day we are born, we begin to make memories that will become our past. Good or bad, that is how life evolves, and, eventually, what makes us who we are. For many people the past becomes their present, as they replay it repeatedly. We cannot change the parts of our life that we now wish were different. We need to accept it as our history, and come to terms with it.

Do not waste another day holding on to any past unhappiness that you may have. You do have a choice to make things better, and happier, not only for yourself but for all those around you. Identify the good in your life. This will give you the encouragement needed to move from the past, so you can truly receive all the gifts that are here for you.

~ Let the past stay in the past ~

People just talk and talk, never realizing what they are saying or how hurtful they can be to those around them. They say mean things, and the old saying, *if you cannot say something nice, than do not say anything at all,* becomes truer. This is a very important step in leading a more positive life and teaching others around you to do the same by your example.

Do not talk too much. Learn to really listen more to what people are saying to you. Be slow to getting angry. Focus on words that you should be saying, and leave out the ones you should not.

~ Choose your words wisely ~

Unfortunately, part of our journey in life is that of loss. Most often when this happens, we suffer in an emotional state known as mourning. This happens to all of us at different stages in our life and from different losses that we endure. The time that we stay in this pattern and carry this emotion varies for every individual. The ultimate result of this is that we can get up and get going again. This does not mean that we forget what it is we are mourning, but we accept that part of our life and start over again.

You cannot continue on wishing, and hoping, that things will change or go back to the way they were before. You have to do your part in making this change, and move on again. Difficult times will always be a part of your life. Loss can be anything from someone moving away, a broken relationship, your ill health, to the death of a loved one. You can make it easier by allowing hope to enter your life again. In addition, you need to make peace with whatever loss you have encountered.

~ Let loss be a part of your life knowing that you can begin again ~

The phrase *practice what you preach,* is one that all of us will hear at some point in our life. We all have our own beliefs, thoughts, and emotions that sustain our everyday life.

It is of utmost importance that we make conscious choices to reflect positive actions. Allow yourself to act upon your own words not by telling but by doing. Try to remember that you are a mentor in this world. You never know who or when someone may be looking to you for guidance.

~ Set an example by doing ~

Forgiveness carries so many emotional ties and can make a person feel whole again. Holding onto grudges, hatred, and feelings of resentment is so negative, as this weighs you down emotionally, physically, and spiritually. Why do so many people choose to live this way? People think that by saying, "I will never forgive him or her," is a way to make themselves feel better and to harm the person who betrayed them. In actuality, it is the exact opposite. This statement of resentment does more harm to that person carrying that vindictiveness than it will ever do to the other person. We relive the negative memory, repeatedly, in our mind, as we build up barriers and feel that pain internally. This is not living a quality life, and the only damage that is being done is to yourself.

Realize that by forgiving someone you are setting yourself free. Free of the pain, the resentment, and the hold that the other person has on you. You gain your life back, and you can live in the present not the past. You can feel peace within yourself again. Then, go one-step further, and forgive yourself for making that choice to let resentment in your life in the first place. Only by allowing yourself to be forgiven, can you begin to heal.

~ Forgive others and forgive yourself ~

Wisdom is in all of us, although some of us may not seem to think that. We live our life in a vicious cycle of enemies. These enemies are known as bitterness, regrets, resentment, hatred, bad attitude, and the list goes on.

Let this never-ending lifestyle go, and seek wisdom. Understand that there will be challenges and hard times in life, but they can all be overcome. You have the ability to do what you want to do by seeking your own inner strength. Make that be the part of you destined for success. Learn from your downfalls, and overcome obstacles that come along during your journey.

~ Have the foresight to move forward ~

Everyone has a story, yet so many of us choose not to listen to one another. We tend to talk over one another and are in a rush to get through to the next thought that is in our mind. We fail to understand that the purpose of communication is to listen, and to understand what someone is trying to get across to us.

Do not be too busy to take the time to listen to what is being said. Be more intuitive, so you can better understand what is being communicated to you. You might just gain more knowledge by becoming a great listener!

~ Stop talking and start listening ~

Life is full of mistakes. It is part of being human and the element of trial and error. As these mistakes come and go we hope to learn something from them. The most frustrating part of making mistakes is when you repeatedly make the same ones expecting different results. Many of my clients say they will never make that mistake again, but time passes, and they are back in the same habitual pattern as previous. When confronted, they always seem to say it is somehow different, or they are in denial that they made that mistake again. Blaming the other person or becoming disillusioned becomes the norm, and they never begin to learn from their mistakes to better themselves.

If you fall into this category and want to live a more productive life, then take the initiative to desire something better and go for it. I hear from parents that they want things better for their children than they had, but I say to them; you are entitled to a life worth living also. Your children will see that you take the steps necessary to make a life that is better for all, and that is the best education you can give them. Eventually, you will find the happiness that you are searching for, and all those around you will learn how to deal with obstacles in the right way.

~ Learn from your mistakes ~

As we have all heard, love is unconditional! However, few of us really know what that means. By loving someone unconditionally, we are saying that we accept that person for whom he or she is, wholeheartedly. Love is not about jealousy or possessiveness. Love allows you to know that the other person is happy because you genuinely care about them.

Love is more than an emotion. It is a way of life, since it can change everything about you and the way you look at life. So, love someone without being judgmental, without limitations, and without restrictions. Give of yourself without expecting something in return, and be truthful. Never harden your heart!

~ Love is the greatest, most rewarding gift you can give and receive ~

Why do some people seem to get more things done or are more accomplished than others are? Is it because they are just lucky? How many times do you come across someone like this and you think to yourself, "If only I could have that or be more like him or her," without ever stopping to think that YOU CAN!

We all have twenty-four hours in a day, but many of us do not realize the importance of time management. Use these hours that turn into days wisely. Go the extra mile, and do not allow foolishness to become the norm. Make the changes necessary to enjoy a full, rewarding life instead of living in unhappiness and stress. Find time in the twenty-four hours you are given, every day, to bring joy and productive thoughts into your life. Stop saying, "I cannot!" and start with, "I can!" and "I will!"

~ If you are not happy, then do something about it starting NOW ~

Being humble can honor all of us if we exercise this trait. Humility is the act of being courteous and respectful of others. It allows us to put someone else's needs before our own, yet still maintain being proud of who we are and what we stand for. However, arrogance and vanity never surface. You do not need to draw attention to yourself by bragging, rather keep a quiet confidence.

A true leader is one who recognizes others for who they are and treats all with respect, regardless of their position. Try listening without judging and appreciating those around you. Also, thank others when they are of help to you. We can always find someone to thank. Do not let that opportunity pass.

~ Humility is highly valued ~

Unfortunately, the norm for most of us is unfulfilled dreams. We put many limitations on our abilities to try to succeed and replace that with fear and anxiety. Our lives then become many broken promises, and unhappiness follows that. Fall in love, educate ourselves, become more successful at work, volunteer, and the list goes on. These are different goals shared by all. However, too often, we do not take the time, nor the effort, to do what is necessary to become the person we desire to be.

Take the time to listen and to look at yourself. See the discrepancy between what you say you want and the reality of what you do. You may be surprised at your behavior. This should not be seen as being hypocritical, since your statements are meant with good intentions. Rather, listen to your words, and put the necessary action into play in order to carry it out. Drop the risk walls, so you can begin to construct your life the way it is meant to be.

~ Action always speaks louder than words ~

Too many people wander through life allowing it to pass them by, as they live in a pity party. The past is relived over and over, and feeling bad, negative thoughts, becomes the norm. This thought pattern and process blocks the mind from all the good things that life really does and can offer us.

Stop living with your head down, and begin to look forward to your everyday life. You have the power and control over all your thoughts! Renew your mind, and make that a daily process. Keep your mind and thoughts positive, so your life will remain that way also. It is never too late, and YOU have the ability to make this happen!

~ Keep your head up while looking forward ~

We search this world thinking someone or something will make us happy. Happiness is the emotion that we all strive to achieve to live a better life. I hear statements, constantly, from clients wishing they were happier. "If I only had _____, then I would be happy." However, what they do not realize is that happiness is a choice. We can choose to stay stuck in our unfulfilling habits and comfort zone, living a life that just gets us by, or we can choose to find within us that longing that will make us laugh again. Not just any laugh, but a laugh so hard that we forget about our fear of change. We allow that silly kid within us to reappear.

You do not need to have the latest and greatest things to be happy. You do not need to worry about what others may think about you because when you do, you allow others to take away from your happiness. Be kind to yourself, and allow happiness into your heart. When you do this, you can share that emotion with others, thereby passing it forward. Read a book, let the sun warm you, play with your children, sit with your partner, smile, don't hold grudges, and find that peace inside of you that has been misplaced for too long.

~ Look at the blessings that you have ~

In this age of entitlement and instant gratification, it is no wonder so many of us forget how to be patient. We lose ourselves by multitasking, over scheduling, and chaos. Eventually, this busyness translates into irritability, restlessness, and disappointment. Nevertheless, it does not have to continue this way.

If there was one trait that all of us should practice, it is patience. Although it takes time to make this a goal in your life, once it becomes habitual, it will be the most valuable asset to you and all those who enter your life. Try to figure out what it is that makes you rush in this world. Slow down, and enjoy your life day by day. Change your attitude about life by letting peace and relaxation enter into your world instead of anxiety and unhappiness. Know that there will be times that will not go your way, and learn to accept that rather than fight it. The time you spend learning patience will reward you in more ways than you can imagine.

~ Patience is a virtue ~

All of us, at some point in our life, will make wrong decisions. This is an inevitable part of our journey. Nevertheless, it does not have to consume us with regrets, thereby never allowing ourselves to move forward. Choices affect you and everyone around you.

Therefore, reverse the wrong decisions you have made in the past. Think before you act or speak. Slow down enough to savor the life that you have been granted. There are NO guarantees that your life will always be a good one, but you can make the right decisions to ensure a better life.

~ Stop producing bad results, so you can start to turn your life around ~

We are surrounded, and consumed, by so many frivolities that we lose sight of the importance of inner peace. There are constant distractions from our cell phones, computers, iPods, headphones, etc., that we become so removed and live in a state of restlessness. Communication and common sense also suffer.

We need to take the time to find our inner peace again, and live a bit deeper. Take every opportunity to find your quiet time as you break down your walls of distractions. Take the time to go beyond your wants, and see what it is you are really feeling!

~ Find out who you are without all the interference ~

Many people in this world live their life in greed. They never seem to have enough, and the desire to want more and more is overwhelming. It affects everyone around them, as that person continues living life in this excessive need. It is a very negative and selfish way to live. Relationships falter, and the bigger, the better becomes the norm.

Do not let greed get a hold of you. Do not allow money to make your decisions. There is no amount of money that will make up for your lack of peace. Yes, money gives you options, but it should never control you.

~ Allow generosity into your life ~

Life can be a series of challenges. All of us react with different stress levels and emotions in order to cope with the demands placed upon us. The greatest coping mechanism we can master is laughter. This can help us to reduce the level of frustration we place on ourselves.

The next time you are in the middle of a difficult or overwhelming situation, try to look at it differently. Do not be so serious that you miss life. Do not be so wrapped up with your day-to-day existence that you forget to smile, let alone laugh. Make a change for you and your health, both physically and mentally. Let the stress melt away with every smile and every laugh. This will become a contagious behavior for all.

~ Do not waste another day without real laughter ~

Just hearing the word *grief* conjures up thoughts of how short life can be as well as the finality of death. We look for answers while trying to figure out how to go on. We are told that things will get better once we gain closure, and we can begin to feel complete again. However, grief does not have to have a time limit, as presented, in order for us to recover.

Grief is something you will go through as you are trying to find your way. It is natural to feel hopelessness, sadness, anger, and despair. However, there comes a time when you need to begin to reconcile yourself to the memories that are left behind. Believe that your life still has meaning. Transfer the love that was left to you back to all those who need you, and make this a permanent change. This is the greatest gift you can give to those you have lost, so they will remain a living presence in you.

~ Let the memories sustain you ~

We spend our days running around making sure that our daily tasks are complete, as we try to build a future with the hope of fulfilling our dreams and desires. We become overwhelmed with our never ending "to-do list," stressing the importance of crossing things off. We struggle with the balance between these two, and, in that, we lose the ability to enjoy our everyday moments.

These moments can be more fulfilling to you if you allow yourself the opportunity to focus on them. These moments make up a fulfilled life because they keep you moving in a forward direction. You need to stay connected, and make each day meaningful. At the end of the day, reflect on your accomplishments, and reconnect with your future achievements.

~ Be present in the present ~

Are you someone who gives up easily? Do you stay in a mindset of *woe is me,* producing negativity wherever you go? You have no goals and no desire to make your life, or others, better. If you have been living this way, then I urge you to begin again.

Stop being so passive. Start to take responsibility for your life and your life choices. Do not be stuck in this mindset. Start doing what you can even if you may think it is not enough. Do not worry about what others may think about you! Make wise choices, and stay determined to make a life worthwhile that includes your talents. Do not miss opportunities!

~ Most of all, do not settle ~

Lacking self-confidence robs you of all your potential abilities, hence success becomes out of your reach. Your life is a constant internal struggle. It is very important that you find a way to feel confident, since it involves every aspect of your life.

There is no quick fix, but you can reach this by self-determination, setting goals, and the focus to follow through. Look at your life now, and think about where you want to go. Take note of your achievements thus far, and be proud of them. Set your goals that will emphasize your strengths. Realize that there will be setbacks, but you have a new mindset that defeats negative self-talk. Create strong mental images about reaching your goals so that success WILL be yours.

~ **Promise to be the best person you can be** ~

Often times, I ask people to tell me about the biggest risk they have ever taken. For some, it is an easy answer: skydiving, facing a fear, running a marathon, etc. However, for others it is a struggle because they are afraid to take a chance. Their emotions get in the way of either trying something new or making a change to their life that will prove beneficial in the end.

Life is short, and we need to put aside our fear of failure in order to get to the next level. If you have a strong desire to do something that will enhance your life's goals, then commit to it and do it. You may surprise yourself, and it may lead you to take other chances in order to better yourself.

~ Venture out of your comfort zone ~

At one point, or another, we run into obstacles and hard times that make us feel stuck in a spiral of bad luck. We feel there is no way to escape this, and, eventually, accept this as our norm. Our lack of motivation and lack of energy to make things better, allows us to continue on this path, never looking for another way out.

When this situation becomes your reality, remember that it is up to you to find a new and different path. Look at the situation that got you to this point so far, and set a new goal of where you want to be. Giving up and staying in this vicious cycle will not allow you to escape. Allow your confidence to take over again in order to move forward in your life. That should always be your goal.

~ Restart your life, and stay focused! You are always worth it~

Uncertainty makes you feel very uneasy and to run from the implications that it holds. It conjures up thoughts of not being in control as events begin to unfold. We would prefer to stay within our boundaries without having things compromised.

However, uncertainty, as we all know, is a part of life. We start new jobs, relationships, and relocate all under this feeling of uncertainty. Instead of making it a negative thought, visualize your future and what the benefits will be with this new growth. Write down all the positives that will occur for you based upon this change. Focus on the outcome of the situation rather than the journey to get there.

~ You know you can do it ~

As we travel on in life, we are faced with new challenges and choices. Some are easier to decide on than others are, but, ultimately, we are the ones who have to make the right decision, or at least we hope it to be. All of us have a purpose in life, and, yet, so many of us struggle with that due to different obstacles that may come our way.

Think about your purpose and role(s) in this life. If you are able to have a clear picture of what it is that you hope to achieve, then follow your passion to make it happen. Remember that there will be struggles along the way, but if you stay decisive then good things will happen. Too many times, you give up as you set out on your life journey, and you lose focus. When this happens, negativity takes place, and your original thoughts become misplaced. You feel hopeless and tend to give up. You live a life filled with disappointment. You must guide yourself to look at the big picture always.

~ Refine your life purpose as you go on, but never let it become abandoned ~

While I was working with a high school senior, preparing her for all the possibilities that lie ahead, she said to me, "I'll never be able to remember this or really know what I want to be." Immediately, following that statement, she began to cry. I said to her, "There is no test that will follow our meeting, only information that you will use to get to the next stage of your life. You have all the courage you need to follow your dreams as long as you always move forward." After some time, she realized what I said was true and that her tears came from fear. Most of her life when things got complicated, or her emotions got the best of her, she gave up, and never thought things were possible.

Many of you choose to live your life this way, always fearing your future and dodging the present. Begin to realize that the only thing that stands between you and your dreams is your will to TRY! Things may be hard in the beginning, but the result will always outweigh that. Keep the faith, and believe that it is possible!

~ **Never give up** ~

Have you ever wondered why some people seem to be very happy, successful, and living their life the way it was meant to be lived, while others seem to be stuck in an unhappy world? If you look at those who are living their life with a definite purpose, you will find that they have a driving emotion known as passion. Not only do they have a sense of how they want to live but, also, they do it with an overwhelming desire and enthusiasm to reach their full potential. That is passion, and it cannot be taught.

Find what it is that makes you passionate enough to embrace all that life has to offer. It may, at first, be met with some type of fear, but go beyond that and pursue it. There are so many possibilities around you, and it is time for you to live the life you imagined. Create a life that you love!

~ **Live your passion** ~

What is your life purpose? Obviously, many of us think about that, but we never fully act upon what we need to do to fulfill our life purpose. Perhaps, it is easier to just give up and continue on the path we have been on. We stay in a **wrong mindset,** and live as if there is no tomorrow. We take no responsibility for our actions, as we blame others for our misery and negativity along the way.

Examine your life. What do you want to accomplish before it is too late? Look at all that you have to offer. You have certain aspects and talent in your life that you can share with others and use in your own life to make things better. Stop wasting your days. Every day you are given another chance to make changes in order to have a great life without settling. Do not miss opportunities to move forward because you allowed laziness to get in the way. Instead, work hard, take responsibility, and make sacrifices to make things happen.

~ Share your life purpose by being the person you were meant to be ~

Plain and simple, reflection should be a constant part of our everyday life. This is so critical because it lets you know what you did and why it worked or did not. Reflection teaches us to learn from our mistakes and what not to do next time. Reflection also shows us the rewards of the good we have done, and keeps us motivated.

Reflection is a powerful learning tool. However, it is up to you to make it a daily habit for a better, more clear-cut life!

~ Lose yourself in thought ~

What is stopping you from forward progress? Are you afraid of change and allowing fear to get in the way? This is how most people live and think. We are so afraid of change that fear takes over, and, when this happens, we run from the unknown. We flood our minds with negative thoughts and emotions instead of confronting it head on with the newness it may bring to us. Then, we begin the pattern of asking others what we should do instead of listening to our own hearts and making our own choices to move forward.

Do not look back. Do not be afraid. Do not give up. You can do this. If the road to your future looks to be a difficult one, so be it in order to arrive at your goal(s). Move forward. You are built for change. That is your constant in this life. You need to challenge yourself, get rid of the bad emotions, and allow your inner strength to take you where you need to go. It is okay to feel afraid, but do not let that stop you from becoming all that you can be!

~ Do not let your fears, or others, stand in your way of moving forward ~

Success is a word that means different things to different people. The one thing it does have in common is that it is something that we strive for in order to have a better life. Success can come in the form of a career advancement, financial stability, weight loss, overcoming an addiction, becoming a better parent, and the list goes on. None of these successes happens overnight, and you need to continue to stay focused until your goal is achieved.

You may stumble, many times, as you are on this path, but continue to work hard at whatever you are going after or change you are trying to implement. Most importantly, always believe in yourself.

~ Stay productive and patient ~

One of the most important gifts we can give to each other is to communicate. The single, biggest complaint I hear from my clients is that they do not talk with each other anymore. Then, emotions build up until it is too late. When confronted, it often ends in arguments, resentments, and relationships gone badly.

I cannot stress it enough how critical it is to communicate often, and state your intentions clearly. Make sure that you are not misunderstood, and give that same respect back to the other person. Effective communication is paramount in order to build trust and secure relationships. This will allow you success in getting along with others as well as being true to yourself. Only you know how you feel inside, so do not make others assume something because you chose not to speak. Let your thoughts flow through your mouth so that you can be heard.

~ Do not hold things in ~

Often, we struggle with unwanted thoughts and emotions that continue to exacerbate. Remember, certain behaviors bring us satisfaction, and use that knowledge to break the struggle of inaction. This way you can end the emotional roller coaster of feeling hopeless and unmotivated. Always look at what you are able to accomplish, and allow those actions and emotions to consume you, which will aid you to feel better.

Be determined, and do not be afraid to fail. Sometimes, your best motivation comes out of failures when you allow yourself to learn from mistakes. Have the courage to begin again, and, each time, gain more momentum to reach that goal which you are striving.

~ Be compassionate to yourself ~

Take things one day at a time. You can turn your life around by doing so and not becoming overwhelmed. You need to look at the whole picture, but you need to step back at times also. Your attitude will always set the course for your daily journey. We all strive for happiness, but we must insist upon joy. Joy will never be found in material items, since it comes from within.

Therefore, keep a positive attitude, and strive for your own inner joy. Do not berate yourself by thinking it is too late to become the person you truly want to be. Opportunity is always out there, but we must put our best foot forward at all times. Be enthusiastic, and take charge of your life. You can choose to be happy, since that is always a choice. Stop living as if you do not have that choice. Be appreciative of all that you have, and, all that you can have, by living your best life. Give thanks daily. No matter what, always start your day off right knowing that you are confident in the path that you are taking.

~ **Live your dreams** ~

How often do you make excuses for not doing what you should be doing or complaining that things are too tough? Are you letting life pass you by, along with wasted talent, all because of a lack of discipline?

Start your day with self-control and the discipline needed to accomplish your goals and tasks. Go the extra mile, and stop wasting your talent. You need to take the initiative to lead a life that you desire and deserve. Do everything with excellence! Always put your best foot forward.

~ Do not settle for mediocrity ~

Your life is created by you and you alone. Yes, others may have an influence towards your actions, and even try to persuade you, if you allow that. However, ultimately, the choice you make is your decision. There is not a person in the world who has the exact same life or thoughts as to what you feel.

Make sure you follow your own intuition, and allow yourself to be in control. Persuasion and temptation will always surround you, but only you have the power to decide which path you will follow.

~ Stay strong and continue to be a leader ~

If I could teach one thing to all, it would be to have a zest for life. Passion for life, for people, and, especially, for living in the present. Unfortunately, this is something that can never be taught. You have to find this for yourself even if you have no clue as to where it might lead you.

I realize that listening to your heart and taking a passionate leap of faith may be that of the unknown, but it is worth it. Do not live your life paralyzed by thoughts that you have nothing to offer. Find something that you are passionate about, and let it free the real you.

~ Take the walls down ~

I am always amazed when I see two people, so afraid, to allow their connection to each other to be heightened by a simple hug. A hug is a way to show a form of affection, or appreciation, to another person no matter what the relationship is. It is not just for those *in love* as too many of us think. We stay rigid to the idea and the contact of it all.

Today, seek out someone who not only deserves a hug but one who could use one. In addition, if someone chooses to hug you because they care about you, then hug them back with open arms. Show them that you too need them, and respect them. A hug is your non-verbal way to tell them.

~ Embrace someone ~

It bewilders me to see how much doubt there is in this world, from the youngest to the oldest. Our society is so full of negativism that people soon believe that they cannot do things or fulfill their dreams. Life becomes dull and full of resentment. We think we do not have the inner capacity to do the things we only dream of.

Stop allowing doubt to kill your dreams. What is it that you would like to do today, tomorrow, or five years from now? If you continue to live in the land of doubt, those dreams will never become a reality! Therefore, begin putting that negative thought aside starting today. Do not wait any longer, and realize that it is possible!

~ **Believe in yourself** ~

Discovery is a powerful word, but we do not realize that we should make this a daily part of our life. We wander through, day to day, doing the same things as a force of habit. Yet, there are so many other things out there waiting for us to discover. There are places to visit, diverse people to communicate with, new foods to try, different hobbies we could take up, etc. However, very few take advantage of discovery.

Start today thinking of something new that you would like to discover, and begin to make that happen. Whatever that may be, write down the steps you will need to fulfill it. Do not let it pass you by without giving it a fair chance to make it come to life. If it is a place that you would like to discover, then make a list of what you need to accomplish that. If it is financial means that are holding you back, then figure out where you can cut corners, or do more, in order for that to become a reality. There are always ways if you allow yourself a time for discovery.

~ Take the leap ~

Celebrate life today in a way you never have before. Do not wait for opportunities, such as weddings or parties, to allow yourself to celebrate the people and events in your life. Choose to celebrate every day that you are here during this journey we call life. It does not have to be on a grand scheme in order for it to be celebratory, but it does have to be a part of you. This exuberance becomes contagious, and the hope is it will spark another to feel this radiant happiness.

Therefore, as you are reading this today, think of what it is you want to celebrate, and do just that. Make this a new part of your life as you start to allow yourself more laughter than tears. It will have a huge impact on all those around you, and, most of all, it will allow you to celebrate your life!

~ You only get one chance at life ~

Why do we put off the things that consume us, mentally, in the hope that tomorrow will be the day to begin? We make to do lists and become stressed out when things are not crossed off the list by the end of the day. In the morning, we wake up with that list staring us in the face.

Instead, begin each day with realistic goals of accomplishing one thing off of your to do list, and if time allots for more, then go for it. If you can achieve at least one action that consumes your thoughts, by the end of the day, then not only will your list become shorter, you will not be on the *I will do it tomorrow* path. You do not have to feel like you have to complete all your tasks, but prioritize. Take it one-step at a time. Things will get finished, and your mind will be at ease.

~ Stop procrastinating ~

"I wish you were never born," "You are so stupid and make me sick," "I hate you and always will," and the list continues. The never-ending words that I have heard from clients to one another, through the years, really hurt the other person so deeply even more so than physical abuse. Yet, these words continue to be said, regularly, by all different people from all different lifestyles. A parent to their child, a spouse to their spouse, siblings to each other, children to their parents or teachers, well you get my point. These powerful words destroy, and they should have no place in your life.

Words always mean something! The words that come out of your mouth should be carefully thought about before being used negatively. Do not feel that it is okay to say these things and then later apologize for them. Those words are *always* remembered. Find another way to express your discontent with another without doing emotional harm. If not, one day, you too will be feeling the pain of it.

~ **Think before you speak** ~

How many secrets are you holding inside that are hurting your everyday existence? We do not realize how dangerous secrets are, and how they can make us feel like we are living in fear. We hold these thoughts deep inside of us and carry them around like dead weight on our shoulders. Sometimes, they are so devastating that we lose sleep. Our concentration on daily tasks is interrupted as well.

If this sounds like something that is stopping you from moving forward, then it is time to share the secret(s) with someone whom you can trust. Talk about it. Try to figure out what happened so that you are not in that position again. Let all the emotions that are associated with that secret out so that you can begin the healing process. If you feel that you cannot talk with someone, or it is just too damaging, then try journaling your thoughts so that you can release the pain via writing. It is more important that you are able to overcome the pain of this carried secret no matter which way is better for you.

~ **Let the healing process begin** ~

Stress is one word that has touched everyone in some way, including good stress. Yes, there is such a thing as good stress, and its correct term is **eustress**. This is a positive form of stress, and it is important for all of us to have in our life.

Eustress allows us to become excited and ready to take on the day without being depressed about things to come. It gives you that euphoric feeling of being alive while looking forward to life's challenges without fear. Try allowing more of this good stress into your life. One way can be by exercising, even if it is a simple walk, or challenge yourself to accomplish one task off your bucket list. Allow an exhilarated feeling to follow you throughout your day.

~ Let eustress be your stress ~

The hardest part of my career has been talking to my clients who have so many abilities, but they choose to do nothing. They come to see me to ask about a plan in order for them to have a better, more fulfilled life. I always want to know what kind of abilities they have or have not. They begin to recite a list containing so much potential, but it is all wasted because they are looking for someone else to do it for them. They clearly have the ability to make it happen. They look for others to blame because of their own laziness.

No one can do it for you. I am not here to be the one to accept you wasting your abilities because you will continue not to succeed. Decide that you are the only one who has the power, and the passion, to make your dreams a reality. Stop waiting for others to come around to make opportunities for your well-being. You must get out there, and make things happen for yourself. There are so many people who have far less abilities than you do, but they do not waste time looking for someone else to make them happy. You have to be the one to work hard, and allow others to see your full potential.

~ Ability only works when you use it ~

Money is something that we all need in order to live in this world; however, it has become the most talked about problem. It is robbing people of life, in general, due to the worry of lack of funds for things that they *want* or *desire*, not things that they truly need. We want the latest and greatest, but it all comes with a cost. I am not talking monetarily.

If you are losing sleep and not enjoying your days because lack of money is eating you alive, then it is time to stop and think about all the time you are losing to these thoughts. If you are driving yourself crazy because you cannot get something you *need*, then it is time to rethink your life. These *needs*, as you might consider them, are really *wants*. In addition, you are proving to yourself that it is more important to lose living in the present by ALLOWING yourself not to live within your means. Move away from these wants. Understand that you are not deprived of things by looking at what you do have.

~ You do not have to have it all ~

During mediation, once again, I hear a spouse say to the other, "I gave you everything," yet the person to whom that quote was directed at had nothing but a blank stare. The other one never gave everything, as it was stated. When I ask what this everything is, 99% of the couples state material items that have been given to their husband or wife. They never even realize that, in the end, none of that mattered. The material items brought them to see me for mediation. The words that were never spoken, or longing for time to be spent together, never happened. Therefore, the *nothing that was given was* the real reality.

We need to be more cognizant about communicating, making memories, and capturing life's moments. A picture can show the beauty but also the ugliness of a memory. Look at your pictures past and present. Now, decide how you want the future ones to turn out.

~ That is the real test to come ~

"I just do not have the time, since I am so busy." How many times have you said that to someone? You shut people out of your life who want communication with you because of this *busy* lifestyle you say you lead, but you have plenty of time to be engaged in social media or to watch your favorite television series. Are you really too busy, or are you just choosing to shut people out until it is convenient for you?

Take the time today even for five minutes, yes, we ALL have that to spare, to get in touch with someone who has been patiently waiting to hear back from you. Better yet, if you can, go visit that person and really brighten their day! You will be surprised how much better you will feel not to mention what joy you may bring another.

~ Hear someone's voice ~

What does the word genuine mean to you? Do you think you are living a genuine life? That is a hard question for most people to answer, since it is not that simple. We all want to think we are a genuine person, but if our lives were to be pulled apart, we would find the answer to be anything but that. We will find that authenticity is not something we practice. We do not accept our weaknesses and live a life that never really feels right.

Stop acting this way, and try to be yourself. Follow your thoughts, and act the way that only YOU know how to act. Accept what strengths and weaknesses you have. That is who you are. Be authentic to your values, beliefs, and, most of all, be accountable. Let the pressures go of trying to be someone you are not.

~ **It is time to get real** ~

A common phone call, which I have been receiving for years, is that of the person who says they need help because they feel like they are constantly in a roller coaster state of emotions. The daily difficulties were becoming too much for them to handle, and they needed a way to get off this so-called ride. The common ground with all of these clients was that they continued to live life in an avoidance state, instead of facing issues head on. Some would turn to substance abuse, while others would continue to live in denial. This is their coping mechanism so that the pain they are feeling never will surface.

Emotions are a part of all of us, as human beings, but running away from them, or riding the emotional roller coaster, will never resolve anything. Face the emotions that you are feeling, and be accepting of the reasons that you feel this way. Do not run from them, or mask the pain. Have the courage to live your life without putting blinders on. You will begin to move past all of this.

~ **Live life with your eyes open** ~

How wonderful life is that we are given a chance to begin again with the promise of a sunrise. The only problem is that too many of us do not use a new day to make changes to a life that may not be going the way we would like it to be. Instead, we complain, and we repeat how unhappy we are. We forget the fact that we do have the power, and the brains, to make our dreams come true.

If you are living a life that is not fulfilling your needs, then make a conscious decision to begin again. You have the internal mechanisms to allow your dreams to become a reality along with the hope and promise of a new day. Do not wait any longer to create a better future. Use your God given brain to make educated decisions to get where you need to be.

~ Let this new day be the day ~

Sadly, I see people treat strangers better than they treat their own family and friends. They smile at them, engage in conversation, and even help them with tasks. However, when it is time to go home to their loved ones, they barely say hello. They grumble about life and become so involved in their own world that there is no effort made to give their home life any time. They are begged for attention.

If this sounds familiar to you, it is about time for you to look at what you are doing to those around you. No one should have to plead with you to have time with him or her. Smile, and be thankful for your family and friends without making them feel less important. Take the time to talk with them daily, and be interested in their life the way they are about yours.

~ Be connected to all ~

How often do you rehash the same things over and over? The never-ending story of negative events that happened becomes the normal conversation, day after day, as if things are going to change by speaking about it forever. I am here to tell you it will never change the outcome. Nevertheless, it will change people's thoughts about talking with you, since they are worried that they may say something to trigger that negativity.

Let it go. The past is the past, and it needs to stop being rehashed. We all understand hard times, but the truth is that is what life is about, taking the bad with the good. I am not saying not to ever discuss it because that is not fair either. What I am saying is that after you have spoken with those that you wanted to communicate with, and they have listened, then it is time to let it go. No one wants to hear the same thing repeatedly.

~ Drop it ~

Relationships are so complicated, but what is worse is when we say things out of anger to another person. We are so caught up in the moment, and things are said that we know deep down inside we do not mean to say. This happens because we are hoping to hurt the other person the way they have hurt us. Anger takes over, and, for some of us, we do not even realize what we are saying at the time. This pattern of hurting another with nasty words will only continue to break down the relationship you are trying to build.

Perhaps, the next time something, or someone, bothers you enough to have that anger start to build inside you, think before you speak. The communicative rage that you want to lash out with will never make the situation better. Ultimately, you need a way to repair this bothersome issue without causing further damage by hurtful, degrading words. You can communicate your frustration without using those kind of words. Practice that the next time this comes into play. It may take more than one try, but you can make anger become positive.

~ **Give it a try** ~

Misunderstandings are very common in any relationship. So, why do you allow them to ruin your days because you choose not to make things better? You live your days as a **right** fighter instead of looking at the whole scenario. The other person's thoughts, or feelings, rarely are taken into consideration, and you spend your time waiting for that apology.

Try to put yourself in the other person's shoes, and see what it is they were trying to get across. At the very least, you can begin to understand what it is they were trying to say or do, and perhaps from there a mutual understanding can exist. When we continually think we are the one who is right and the other one is wrong, then we do not allow others to be who they are. Finally, you should be able to work together instead of trying to decide who is right and who is wrong.

~ Be mutually beneficial ~

How often do you allow doubt to disallow your hopes and dreams for a better tomorrow? You trade your future for skepticism, questioning and second-guessing thoughts you are having. Instead of following through with plans you have, you let them go because you stop believing in yourself.

Self-doubt can be conquered by embracing who you are and what you stand for. You do not need others to pat you on the back and help you to move forward. You need to do that on your own and not have to have others praise you for what you are trying to do. Praise yourself knowing that you are full of confidence and self-esteem. Doubt should never enter your life as you continue to shine.

~ **Believe in yourself** ~

I saw a child imitate their parent so well, yet it was so disturbing. She was only six or seven years of age. She was yelling at her little sister saying, "Shut up you dummy, and sit still," while her mom was on the phone. I was outraged watching this learned behavior. I realized that people still do not understand just how contagious the art of imitation is and the impact it has on children. We want our children to act a certain way; however, when they act what they see, we are quick to judge them and label them as **bad.**

Instead, how about you realize that your every step is being monitored and role modeled. Are you doing the things that you want others to imitate, or will you shudder when you see them? Do not demand **right** from others when all they see is **wrong.**

~ Choose to be the positive model ~

Apathy is a word that I truly dislike because there are so many people who live this way. I see this from the young to the old, and this should not be. Do I need to remind you that it can be defeated and replaced with more positive emotions in life? Life should not be lived emotionless or non-caring.

You have the freedom to choose the attitude that you want to carry no matter what the situation is. Tomorrow everything could be taken from you, so why choose to live with a lack of interest towards life. No matter what curve balls are thrown at you, you have the choice to make it better, and no better time than the present.

~ Take action to release apathy ~

I have always lived by the motto that **life is not a dress rehearsal**, and, for most of you, I am sure you have at least heard that saying once in your life. The problem is few of us live by these words until it is too late. Think of all the people you know who keep doing the same things, never getting to where they want to be in life. They grumble and moan, never taking the next step to complete even a simple task. Days turn into weeks into months into years. Then, we realize that we have wasted all this time as if it were practice for our **real** life.

Wake up everyone. Stop allowing yourself to wait for the perfect moment or the exact right time to take a leap of faith. That is not how it works. You may find that day will never come. Life is about living, and not acting as if you have unlimited time. You have limited time! Start making moments count, and stop practicing for a tomorrow.

~ Time is ticking now ~

How quick are you to judge someone from first impressions? You may not like what they say, or how they look, because they do not conform to your standards. However, did you ever consider what it is they may have gone through, or may be going through, to get them to that point?

Today, instead of quickly criticizing someone, take the time to introduce yourself, and learn a little something about him or her. That co-worker who you always talk about behind their back, a student in your class that you pick on, or even a cashier at your local grocery store are all people with stories to tell. They have a history just as you do. Allow them to speak for themselves before you quickly decide that they are strange.

~ Do not judge a book by its cover ~

The big buzzword we are constantly hearing about is that of gratitude, which is interesting since few of us actually allow that to be a part of our lives. We walk around complaining about what we do not have and how it is not fair that others may have more. The bigger picture is still not seen, and it makes me wonder if it ever will.

Be thankful for all that you have and all that you have been given. Instead of whining about what you do not have, say thanks with an appreciation for all that you do have. Realize that in life you may never have all that you desire, but what is your reality now should be held with the utmost gratitude.

~ Give thanks ~

"I am not good enough," "I do not have the talent," "I will just fail at that," and "I am not smart enough."

If this sounds like you, then I beg you to stop saying those statements. Realize that not only do you have the wherewithal to make a difference, but also you are good enough. Stop allowing others to stand in your way and make that decision for you. Let your potential out instead of wasting it. People who truly care about your well-being will stand beside you, and the rest need not be listened to.

~ **Stand up for you** ~

My toughest challenge with clients has been to teach them that the art of WORRYING GETS YOU NO WHERE. No matter how many times I speak of this, little change takes place. I understand that it happens for a multitude of reasons, but I have yet to see that your worrying will change the outcome of that situation. I know that as you are reading this, you are agreeing with that statement. You know, firsthand, that all your worrying never did change the situation. It may feel like you are being productive, but it is the exact opposite.

Therefore, the next time that an occurrence arises and you feel the need to worry, try doing something else to pass the time. Call a friend or family member, exercise, read, listen to music, dance, or write in your journal, anything other than the non-productive worry session. It is possible to heed worry off in another direction. Remember, worry will never change the outcome, but it will change you.

~ Get off of the rocking chair of worry ~

Negative people will only bring you down, thus why do you stay friends with people who continually live their life this way? Their negativity will never help you to be more positive, and your environment will become more toxic. A dark cloud will feel like it is looming over you, and you cannot understand why you keep allowing this to happen to you.

It is time; no, it is passed time, for you to seek out others who choose to have a positive outlook on life. Not only will that help you, but also your environment will be more open to being surrounded by people who have an interest in you. They have a zest for life, and this becomes contagious to all around you. It is much easier to move forward when you feel positive energy than to feel like your feet are in quicksand surrounded by negativity.

~ Time is precious ~

How often do you criticize yourself? I look terrible today, my hair looks awful, these clothes make me look fat, everyone is staring at my pimple, and the complaints continue. We all have days like these, but we need to stop being so critical of who we are.

You are given a body, mind, and soul upon birth. It is who you are. You have to accept all of it, and understand how wonderful and blessed you are. We are all individuals and not here to please every person that we meet. Get rid of that inferiority complex. If someone has something to say about you, develop an *oh well* attitude because deep down inside they are struggling with their own criticism of who they are.

~ Belittling yourself is not acceptable ~

Taking care of yourself is so important even though we always seem to make excuses for that. "I cannot," is the common answer to most questions when asked if we did something for ourselves. We have a million excuses as to why we did not, but we have no real reasons.

Take the time for yourself, and make you the priority. If you are not giving it your best, then how can you expect to give your best to someone else? Strive to put your best foot forward today, and do something for you that has been pushed aside for far too long. Maybe you have wanted to read a book, take a walk, or just sit and catch up on all those programs you have been recording. For me, I like to put music on and sit down to write. It feels great, and I am doing something that I want to do.

~ Find something just for you ~

Emotions can sometimes come over us even when we are not expecting them. They can range from fits of laughter to uncontrollable crying. It can happen because of life events, something you may see, or perhaps just a song you are hearing.

No matter why this occurs, be content with your emotional side, and do not feel any kind of embarrassment. It is wrong to think that if you cry, or allow your true emotions to come out, then you are a weak person. In fact, it is the direct opposite of that. Allow your human side to be seen and for you to feel what you want when you want.

~ Do not hold back ~

One of the greatest things you can do for yourself is to face whatever fear you have, so it does not have any more power or control over you. Although, this is easier said than done, it is possible. Growing up I had a fear of broken glass, and, for whatever reason, whenever something made of glass broke, I went into a panic and could not even help to clean it up. In college, I spoke to one of my psychology professors about it, and I started to come to terms with this irrational thought. Fast forward to the time when I had my first child and she broke something. I had to face my fear to clean it up so that she would not step on it and get hurt. It was that day that I released myself from that fear, never allowing it to have power over me again.

What fears are you holding inside? Fears are irrational thoughts and can hold you back from many things, no matter how trivial they may seem to another person. They are your fears, and you need to deal with them in order to release them. If it is something that you can handle on your own, then begin today to set yourself free. If it requires professional guidance, then come up with a plan to make that happen.

~ Stop living your fears ~

Your past can continue to haunt you if you continue to relive it. Yes, there will be past history that you wish would have continued on, but holding on to it is not allowing you to live in the present day. Continually bringing up your past is not helpful in moving forward, and it can drag you down to the point of sadness and depression. Then, the spiral begins, and thoughts of *if only* become a topic of your everyday life.

Stop the cycle today by grasping the fact that you do not get a second chance to do over the present day. You will never be the same age at this moment in time again, so allow that to be your thought process. This very moment in time is for you to make a new memory not destroy present day reliving yesterday. It is done and over. Today holds so much promise for you, but you will never see that if you do not become a part of it. Be excited to share another day.

~ Every day holds a new promise ~

Over the years, I have found more and more people who really feel as if they have nothing to give to this world, let alone live for. They go through their days as if it is a chore, never realizing their true self-worth.

I am here to tell you that you **are** worthy of life and all that it has to offer. Find something that you can really believe in, and stick to it. God gave every individual on this earth a purpose. It is up to you to find out what your calling is. Then, make that your drive to get moving every day.

~ **You got this** ~

It is frightening to see the number of people, of all ages, living on medication, or looking for happy pills, as if that is the answer for a better life. They walk around flat lined and continue living a conflicted life with unsatisfying routines. Happiness is replaced by despair. These pills are not effective at making them happy. It is up to us to find our joy in life, and that does not come from medication.

Start showing up for life! Take small steps to improve your quality of life. You can have hopes and dreams, but, without any real action, they will only continue to be words and thoughts. Get more out of life by trying new things, and let go of boredom. It is hard to be unhappy when you surround yourself with something to look forward to.

~ Get motivated ~

Many people feel that two wrongs make a right. I absolutely disagree with that statement and believe that you should never live that way. You are acting on the same behavior, in the same way, as the behavior that you did not like in the first place. It does not get you anywhere.

Please rethink this thought, and stop acting on impulse because another person did that same thing to you. You know it does not get you anywhere, and it certainly does not change unwarranted behavior. Always think before you act, and never stoop to another person's wrongdoings. You know in your heart, and head, that it is all wrong. You are only making yourself look bad, for no reason at all.

~ **Make better choices** ~

One of the greatest joys in my life has been raising my children and seeing them grow as individuals. More specifically, is the way that every day was a new beginning to them especially when they were younger. It did not matter what happened the day before because the dawn of a new day brought a completely new world of opportunity.

I ask you to take today as a day of new hope, and a chance to begin again. Look at the world differently, and not as though it owes you something. Be innocent as a child is, and notice all the good around you. If you have been taking people for granted, then stop that behavior. They will not be here forever. Then again, neither will you. Remember that!

~ Let innocence back into your life ~

I constantly see or hear someone who is stressing over the smallest things possible. You have heard it frequently not to sweat the small stuff, but you continue to live life this way. All the joy that could be in your day is overshadowed by this insignificance. You get angry at things such as: misplacing your keys, a store sold out of your favorite food, waiting in line to check out, and the list continues. The stress you are putting on your body is not worth it. In addition, it will not make these things change for the better.

However, you can change this behavior with some practice. You can be the person who takes things in stride instead of blowing up over these mundane incidences. It is called **reasoning.** You need to use your part of the brain that is responsible for this instead of allowing your negative emotions to surface, resulting in anger and irritation. Therefore, the next time an unimportant issue arises, try to look at it as a chance to reason what is going on and not a life or death situation. Realize that there will always be small setbacks on your journey, but you have the ability not to allow it to take over your life or let it ruin your day at all. Regulate your emotions to look at the small things with a shrug it off attitude.

~ Learn to be even-keeled ~

There are no guarantees in life, but every choice we make will create our journey, good or bad. By making the right choices, we can stay on a positive track for a more successful life.

Stop wishing for things to come your way. There are those of us who continue to wish, and those of us who get out there and DO!

~ Stand up and be a DOER ~

Many negative thoughts, stories, and people encompass us. The news is always covering stories of despair and agony. They frighten, place panic, and overwhelm us at times. Sometimes, good stories are told at the very end, but the majority of people cling to the bad. Is this a representation of your thoughts? Do you cling to negative thoughts instead of looking for joy in your life?

You can have all the joy and happiness you would like, but it will take some time and work. My clients are told to write down their thoughts, or, if they do not want to write, just draw the emotions they are feeling each day. At the end of the week, look back and see if there are more positive than negative emotions. Take your negative thoughts and turn each one into a positive one by figuring out how to make that change. Do not say someone is preventing your happiness or that you need material things to make that happen. That is the farthest thing from the truth. The answer is that your thoughts are preventing your happiness, so find out how to turn your negative thoughts and issues into positive, productive ones. Make the effort to make the changes. It is worth every second of your time you put forth.

~ Your happiness depends on it ~

Do you know people who constantly change who they are depending on the person they are around? Is that person you? If it is, then it is time to get real. Time to see the person you have become and all the hats you are choosing to wear just to fit in. It becomes exhausting to live that way, and no one ever knows who you really are.

Be yourself. You are the only one who knows you, and you need to love yourself for that person. Do not try to live for other peoples standards, as you compromise who you are. This is not an authentic way to live. You are trading your thoughts and actions, as you continually lose your identity. Be proud of what you stand for! Do not let anyone bully you into thinking otherwise.

~ Be authentic ~

How wonderful it is to have a best friend. They are there for us through good times and bad. We can depend on them for anything, and our love for them is unconditional. Some of us are lucky enough to find at least one person in our lifetime that we can call our best friend. Some of us have several. Still, the best friend that many of us never have is ourselves.

Reacquaint yourself with you. Stop putting yourself down, and start to announce to yourself what a great person you are. The insecurities you have are all from within yourself and are not necessary. Love who you are. You do not need to rely on others to make you feel whole. You have the power to feel complete.

~ Be your own best friend ~

We are all in this journey together. None of us will get out of it alive. Even though this is the case, too few of us even try to get to know other people, and allow mutual respect to be a part of our world. I am not saying that you have to agree with everything that someone else may believe or think, but I am asking that you at least allow the differences.

Make today the day you get to know someone else. Take the time to talk with someone who may be in your apartment building, a neighbor down the street, a student in your dorm or class, or the same person you see at the grocery store weekly. You may find that you have similarities. If nothing else, you may have taught another person to pass it forward, and reach out to another human being.

~ Connect with someone new ~

What is your escape plan? I do not mean the one in case of fire, but the plan to let the everyday struggles be put on the back burner for a short time. A time for you to reconnect, and have time for yourself.

There are countless ways to do this; meditate, go for a walk, a drive, read, take a ten-minute time out, write, and the list goes on. I like to listen and sing to music that allows me to escape in my thoughts. By no means am I a world-class singer, but it is so gratifying to get lost in song. I forget about everything else and feel refreshed. Now it is your turn. Find your bliss in this world where you can escape totally, for a short period, before you begin again. It is good for the mind, body, and soul.

~ **Lose yourself** ~

Our journey consists of several roads that we travel on while working our way to our destination. Sometimes, we reach our goals with no bumps in the road. While other times, it becomes a dead end. We feel lost, hopeless, and even abandon our dreams when the latter road becomes our reality. We think it must not have been meant to be.

You need to recognize that the rocky roads you will have to get across are not meant to be a sign to give up. Look at the journey through that course, and learn from the mistakes or choices that were made along the way. You are not lost because of this wrong turn. Rather, it is a teaching tool for you to see where it is you are going. Every road you travel, on your journey, is a learning experience, both the good and the bad.

~Do not abandon your destination when you feel lost~

Do not cry over something or someone who will never cry over you! They do not deserve your tears. There will be people you meet or things you may truly want that make you cry, but it is to no avail. You are wasting your time, energy, and your emotions.

Find the people who will be there for you, at all costs, who would never bring you to the point of tears. Many people will help you and make you feel at ease, even in times of distress. Those are the people you should take comfort in knowing your relationship with them will not make you cry.

~ Do not waste your tears ~

Having a broken heart is such a painful experience, but, at the same time, it is very rewarding. I know this may sound like an oxymoron, but if you can say that you have had this feeling, at least once, then it means you have taken a real risk in life.

Life is about adventure and risk taking, and I am here to tell you that all of it is worth it. Even a broken heart is worth the pain. I have had my share of broken hearts, and, with each of them, I have learned to love even harder and to go the extra mile. The disappointment that you will feel, as I have, means you allowed yourself to try something. Of course, a broken heart can be from loving someone, but it can also be from a goal that you wanted to achieve, a friendship gone wrong, or the death of a loved one. Nevertheless, all of these instances are worth the risk involved and, yes, even a broken heart.

~ **Care deeply** ~

Some form of emotional pain will inevitably enter your life. When you are going through this period, it feels like forever. You spend your days wondering if and when it will ever pass. You begin to believe that it never will, and the saying *there is light at the end of the tunnel*, is meant for everyone except you.

If you could learn one thing, and, always remember, it is that everything in life is temporary and does pass. The distraught feelings will eventually lessen, and the pain will decrease. After this ordeal, you will have an awakened sense of life, and new thoughts will emerge. Use this heightened sense to grow, and move forward.

~ **Nothing is ever permanent** ~

Our world can be an amazing place, but it is always up to us to find the good in it. There are plenty of people, I am sure you know, who are constantly living on the negative side of life. They try to get as many people to agree with them and be on their side as they can. They go about this determined to make others feel as depressed as they are and to have them join in their never-ending hymn of complaints.

Now, do not get me wrong, there are many problems and bad things in this world, but it is always up to you to find the positives. I choose not to ignore the bad things as if they do not exist, but I am not going to dwell on them so that my existence will not move forward. I have problems also, since I am only human. The difference is that I try to find even the smallest bit of unambiguity in my everyday life. Then, I go one-step further by trying to make it better for the people around me. It is not hard to live this way.

~ Try to make the world a better place ~

What will happen to you when you come to the crossroads of life? Will you know which road or direction to choose to lead you to the happiness that you are longing for?

The answer is that when you do reach a crossroad there are no guarantees that the road you choose will be the right one. You have no idea where or what that will lead you to. You choose it in the hopes that it is the right one. You may be so in love with someone, but his or her love is not reciprocated back. You may be extremely successful in your career, but you still feel alone. There are no written guarantees that the choices you make will always be the right ones; however, continue to make them instead of running from them.

~ That is what life is about ~

I believe that everything that happens to you is done on purpose and a direct correlation as to your actions, past and present. You may feel like running away from your problems, your failures, your relationships, and your heartaches, but that is never going to help you with moving forward.

I urge you to look at all the negatives in your life, and use them as learning tools. Why do you feel like nothing is ever right in your life? Did you ever stop to look at how you got to that point? Take some time to trace the steps that brought you to feeling this way. Now, look at those steps again from an educational point of view. Learn from them in order to be successful instead of feeling as if you are a failure. You are never a failure! That is the first place to start. Accept you, and take the first step to self-improvement.

~ **You can have self-success** ~

A friendship is an awesome relationship, but it can also be a very uncomfortable situation. You keep surrounding yourself with people who constantly berate you, or they make you not feel like yourself. You come home feeling so emotionally drained. You keep telling yourself that you are done with them, only to hang out with them on another occasion.

If any of this sounds like your so called friends, then, by all means, have the strength and courage to let them go now. You should not be struggling with feeling less than whom you are when you are together with them. That is not a friend. A friend will allow you to be you, and any connection that does not fulfill that should be non-existent. You are nothing less than great. Find those who make you feel that way, and encompass those people as friends.

~ A friendship should never feel forced ~

Divorces truly bring out the material items in my clients, and I still struggle watching them define themselves by their stuff. Constantly having to show off to their family, friends, and their neighbors as if these things make them the person they are. A material life should never define you. You are giving your life away to be and act a certain way, and this is nothing less than a tragedy.

Look in the mirror, and tell me that your stuff is what you are made of. I guarantee it is not. However, I can say that you are made of emotions, hopes & dreams, desires, thoughts, family, friends, apprehensions, and opportunities. Stop allowing the bigger and the better, not to mention marketing, to overtake your life to the point that items define it. Life is about meaning and experiences.

~ Do not define yourself by trying to impress ~

Time is so very precious! Please stop waiting around for others to give you an approval to move forward. I know some people become fixated on the need to have someone approve of what it is that they are doing or thinking.

Do not allow someone else to tell you how to be successful, happy, or, ultimately, how to live. That is your job, and waiting for the okay from another person is wasting your time. You are the **best** and **only** person who should be making your decisions for a better future, while living in the present.

~ You do not need anyone's permission ~

My life has been enhanced because of the awesome and ever growing technological world that we live in. I enjoy using my smart phone, my computer, and my surface. I am sure many of you can say the same, but you also need to take the time to stay focused in life. These advances are valuable in many ways; however, we are becoming too addicted that we are missing life.

We do not even take the time to see what is going on in our everyday life. We are so involved in our cyber worlds. People are not talking to one another when they are sitting right next to each other. Instead, they are texting one another or are involved in watching something else on one of their screens. Life is just passing them by. No real connections are being made. You need to disconnect, and become focused on your life and the people within it. You may feel that you are staying connected with all these other friends online, but the people who are standing right in front of you are being neglected. Take your eyes away from whatever device you are on, and engage with your family and friends in real time, real life, and vocal conversations. They deserve you to be a part of their life, all the time, not just when you feel like disconnecting from your screen. Stop allowing life to pass you by. You cannot get the time back.

~ Refocus on your real life ~

As I said earlier in this book, passion is not something that is taught. It has to be felt internally. I cannot teach you that. On the same hand, I cannot make you appreciate all the good that you have in your life. It is up to you to fully grasp and remind yourself that in order to have true happiness you must also learn to appreciate all that you have. When you allow your mind and your thoughts to wander, thinking the grass is greener somewhere else, then you lose your focus of what your life has become and all the greatness that is in it.

Therefore, take the time to acknowledge what you have and where you are going. Do not wait until it is too late and you lose the people and things that you were complaining about in the first place. Make provisions now to be cognizant about how wonderful your life really is, before it is over.

~ Do not wait, appreciate ~

Never take things so personally. It is my experience that people who criticize another person do so because that is what someone did to them. You need to understand that so that you do not start to harden your heart because of the indignity of another human.

Allow yourself the freedom not to allow other people, who may criticize you, to affect your well-being. You should always continue to take the high road, and be the better person without it becoming a personal attack. Taking things personally will affect you negatively, which cause you to put up internal barriers towards others. Do not allow this to become a part of you or to define you.

~ Free yourself from the hurt ~

How do you respond in tough situations? Do you become extremely angry and react with road rage when someone is not driving the way you would like him or her to drive? If you are at a restaurant and you have to wait too long to be seated, do you start an aggressive demand? Do you really think that your anger is solving the problem? There are so many daily situations that you will come across, but the main thing is to learn to deal with them using a different approach other than aggression.

The next time a rough situation occurs, try to stay calm instead of allowing rage to be the norm. People will react and respond to you more favorably than when you act with lunacy. You can still say what you want to say, but use a different tone that will allow for possible change without sacrificing your goodness.

~ Try a different perspective ~

I am not only a believer in performing acts of kindness but I practice that every chance I get. It is so rewarding to see another person's face when you help him or her with something. There is nothing better than the euphoric feeling it will also award you.

I hope that you will try a random act of kindness, at least once, and see the benefits that all parties involved will receive. It will make you feel good inside, and, perhaps, it will spark another person to pay it forward as well. What is better than that!

~ Practice kindness ~

Emotions can sometimes get the best of us, and when it becomes so difficult to control your emotions, it can lead to toxicity. This toxicity is seen in people who just flip out over everyday issues. For example, raging at your child for spilling cereal all over the floor, screaming at a retail employee for a mistake they made, losing it because your mechanic said it would only take sixty minutes and now they need more time, and the list continues. Does any of this sound familiar?

If you find that you cannot control your temper, crumble with tears over the smallest things, and really cannot manage your emotions, then it is time for some assistance. There is help for you to get control again even if you feel you have exhausted personal means. You need to find the underlying culprit to all of this, and learn how to deal with the real problem that leads you to this point. Do not be ashamed. You just need some support and guidance to redirect these actions.

~ Get control over your emotions ~

Spending quality time with family and friends should always be a priority in your life. I know that we all have things that take us away from each other for hours, and sometimes days at a time, but you need to make time to be around those that care about you. So many of you are caught up in your work world that when it comes to family time, you are so stressed, exhausted, and overworked, that no enjoyment can be had. It takes a toll on all of those around you.

Time is too priceless to keep allowing this to be your way of life. You need to find a way to work less, make better choices, or simplify your life in order to find a balance for all. Make the choice to show that you are willing and able to be there for your family. Stop missing everyday life and many "firsts" that will never happen again. Your spouse wants time with you, but not surrounded by your drifting thoughts. Your children want you to see them and know them for the people they are becoming. Time is slipping by. When all is said and done your work will not be there begging for you back, but your loved ones will.

~ Enjoy the part of your life that truly matters ~

It is very important that you realize that you are not the end all, be all, in this world. There is a connection to all of your existence.

You have a soul and a purpose in this world. Connect with your spirituality or religion to find your true purpose. You can do this by belonging to an organized religion, practice private prayers, or meditation. Whatever you choose, it is just important that you do something.

~ Be spiritual ~

Perfection is a concept that never really exists. As you know, we are not perfect people nor do we live in a perfect world. However, we continue to search for the perfect everything in our life. We want to find the perfect companion, job, friends, and even a house. None of these things will ever exist because we are constantly changing. Therefore, nothing stays the same. The person you thought was perfect for you yesterday is not the same way you feel today.

Instead of looking for perfection in your life, keep an open mind. Look at the person you are with, and see the sincere and devoted relationship you have. Allow your job to blossom into a career that you are proud of, and look to your friends as a comfort to you, even in the darkest of times. Make your house into a home by adding your touches to it to make it a place of comfort. All of these things can be conquered when you let go of the perfection you think you will find.

~ Perfectionism is nonexistent ~

Finding a balance in life should be a priority. When I meet my clients for a consulting session, I ask them what they want out of life and how are they achieving those goals. Of course, happiness, finding true love, money, and having more time are always on the top of the list. Now, when they are to answer if they are achieving these goals, hesitation always plays a part. There is no balance in their life. Sound familiar?

The reason for this non-balance is that you are allowing one area of your life to be consumed, always, which leaves no time for anything else you are looking to accomplish. You can have all the right goals but if your social life is what takes up the majority of your daily time, then how can you devote any time to another area in your life? It becomes impossible. You start to feel that something is missing from your life. Do not allow this to keep going on. Choose all the areas in your life that you want to concentrate on, and balance them out amongst your days, weeks, months, and years. Do not neglect one area of your life because you have allowed another area to take over. You can get all things accomplished in your lifetime with a balance.

~ Do not trade one for the other ~

Gossip and drama are two realities that will never bring about a productive life. You spend time talking about others and making things worse than they actually are. Talking badly about others, even those you care about, becomes the norm. In addition, you surround yourself with other people who are acting the same way. It is a nasty way to live, and, eventually, you hurt too many people.

Get away from this chain reaction. If you want to discuss other people, then speak of the good. Choosing to communicate negatively about others and/or listening to it from others will only stimulate negativity in your life. Make today the day you say enough of all this gossip and drama. Say good-bye to that part of your life. Let those people go who continue to speak and act that way. You do not need to do this any longer.

~ Walk away from all of it ~

I had a friend that always thought about the worst-case scenarios in her life. If she had a little cut on her hand, then she was sure it would turn into a terminal infection. If she went on a trip, she was sure someone was going to try to rob her house while she was away. She allowed her mind to be so preoccupied with events that are not very likely to happen. This negative mind set has now replaced her happier thoughts. She became so full of doubt that nothing made her happy anymore. It was very hard to see that evolve.

If you live in a constant state of distrust and ambiguity, you really need to let that negativity go. You are allowing your life to slip away. Make the choice to let positive thoughts enter your mind, and replace the negative ones. Open your eyes to the good that is out there, and allow enthusiasm back in. You have the capability to be joyous.

~ Replace your lack of faith ~

Are you present when you are around people you care about? If you were to leave the room, or to be gone for an extended period, would those people miss your absence? If you can answer yes to both of those questions, then keep up the good work! If you cannot say that, then make it right.

Begin by giving your full and complete attention when you are interacting with others. Show them that they are of the utmost importance to you and that distractions will not be part of your time together. The most important thing is the time that you are spending at that moment. Do not begin thinking of the next thing that you have to do. Giving your undivided attention, and time, to your family and friends is the best legacy you can leave. You will always be remembered and appreciated for that.

~ Stay present in the presence ~

Imagine if today was the last day you ever saw a loved one. Obviously, we have no way to know that, nor do we want to think like that. The unfortunate truth is that someday that will be the reality for us. We may not get the chance to express our true sentiments to the people we love so much.

Please be more cognizant of this. Begin to tell loved ones how much they mean to you and how grateful you are for them. I know you may be thinking that they already know this, but what does it hurt to say it more frequently. Any chance you get to remind someone of the depth of your love for them, take it. Do not let another moment pass because you may not get another opportunity. Life is full of tragedies. Then, sadly, we are slapped in the face with the reminder of how short life really is.

~ Do not wait until it is too late ~

Relationships can be very complicated along with issues that seem overwhelming. You begin to talk with everyone and anyone who will listen. I even see people posting their problems on social media. They hope that people will see their issues and take their side. This is not the way to make a relationship or your dilemmas work out. This is a very bad ploy at airing your dirty laundry and a way to get some sort of attention.

Your relationship issues will not be worked out this way. The only way to make this happen is to talk with the other person involved, and work it out with them. Other people should not be allowed to be pulled into your business. You should never air your resentments for the world to see. They do not know anything about your relationship, so stop relying on them for any kind of advice.

~ Talk it over with the involved person ~

I attended a funeral for a friend, and the number of people attending was mind blowing. The church was not even able to hold all the people. They had to leave the side doors open to allow all to hear. As I sat there, tears falling, I realized that this is the reality of what I preach, and, yes, I practice. You see, he was kind to people he met, did not burn bridges, and tried to see people for who they were, not for what they could give him. He loved people unconditionally, and he did not hold grudges. He wanted to leave the world a better place than he found it, and, I realized sitting there, he did just that. Many people I knew. However, some attendees were just acquaintances from a chance meeting with my friend, but they came because he touched their life in a meaningful way. They will miss that interaction. The majority of the comments I heard were that they would miss his smile, his love for life, his unconditional love for people, his heartfelt messages, but most of all, his positive attitude. How very touched I was as were all of us.

At the final moment, it was very clear how he lived his life because there was standing room only. That was his legacy. Therefore, I ask you…

~ How will you make your ending ~

ABOUT THE AUTHOR

Gina M. D'Amore-Nisco's educational background is in Psychology. She is a Divorce and Conflict Resolution Mediator, Independent Educational Counselor, Life Strategies Counselor, Certified Stress Management Coach, Certified Corporate Wellness Coach, and Entrepreneur. Her methods, approach, techniques, and ideas have been proven effective to all those that she has helped in the past, and for future clients yet to benefit from her expertise.

Gina is the founder of Positive Next Steps and is immensely humble to all of her clients that continue to seek her out for her guidance, professionalism, and knowledge. Gina assists parents and their children with the entire college process, mediates both divorcing parties in order to come to mutually beneficial terms, and helps others set a plan to reach their life goals. She is a leader in her field and will continue to assist those who want to live the life they imagined!

Gina M. D'Amore-Nisco is available for workshops and lectures. Details will be sent upon request.

To contact Gina please visit her website at: **www.positivenextsteps.com**

JOURNAL PAGES

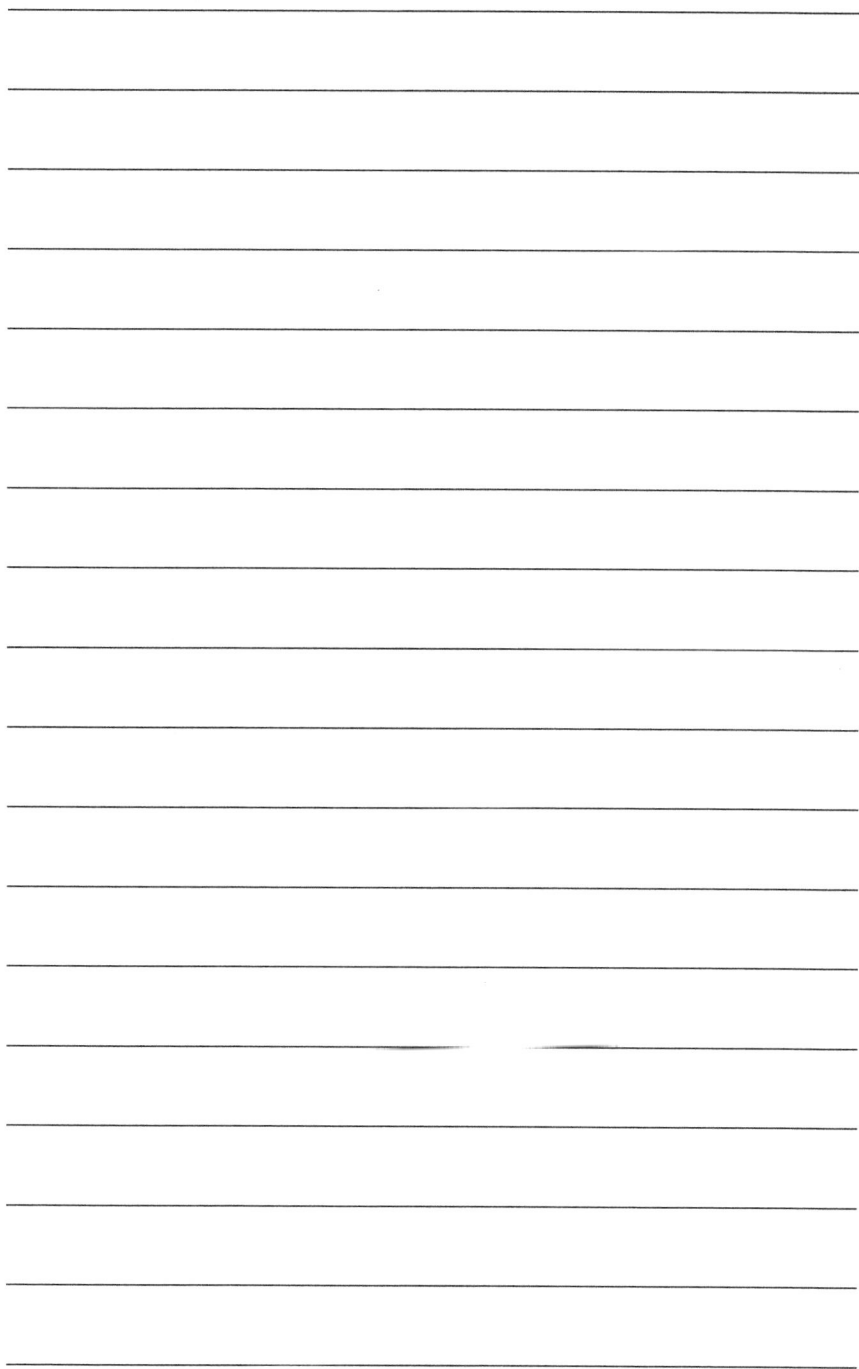

www.ingramcontent.com/pod-product-compliance
Lightning Source LLC
Chambersburg PA
CBHW060301050426
42448CB00009B/1714